Codes of Light

The Golden Codes of Shamballa

Spiritual numbers to uplift humanity and multiply

all the energies of love, light, and happiness

Georgios Mylonas

Geom!*

Important Note
The recommendations made in this book should not be considered
a replacement for formal medical or mental treatment. A physician
should be consulted in all matters relating to health, including any
symptoms that require medical attention.
Anyone who has emotional, mental, or physical problems should
seek professional consultation before attempting any of these
practices.
While the information and the suggestions in this book are believed
to be safe and accurate, the author cannot accept liability for any
harm as a result of the use or misuse of these practices. This book is
intended as general information and for educational purposes.

Geom!*
Georgios Mylonas: teacher and author of methods of energy healing,
personal development, and spiritual advancement

School of Reiki, Athens

www.energiesoflight.com
www.universityofreiki.com
www.reiki.gr

e-mail: reiki@reiki.gr

Translated by Anastasia Christidou

ISBN: 9608960614
ISBN 13: 9789608960619

10 percent of proceeds go to charity

Eden!

Approach the Golden Codes of Shamballa, apply and use them, and receive all of their abundant, wonderful, and magnificent gifts in a state of gratitude with humility and respect. Proceed with love—the greatest love you can sense and feel, the greatest love you can become and be. Meditate and work with the golden codes in an expanded, heightened, positive state of mind, keeping your spirit and heart open, warm, generous, and radiant. Follow the purest, the highest intention. This primary intention exists within, in the ultimate and supreme spiritual world of light that is found within you, within your soul—your Eden.

Be Aware!

You are about to change. You are already changing. You will experience major and minor changes, and all of them will be positive and good in nature, in their essence. Keep in mind, there is a very high probability that the Golden Codes of Shamballa will bring forth the best of you—the greatest, the highest of you. Right now, it is more probable than ever that you will encounter and possibly enter the all-encompassing, all-transcendental, ecstatic blissful happiness for which Shamballa, the spiritual dimension, is best known!

Energetic Attunement!

This work is dedicated to the whole of humanity, to every single human being. To all, to you, with love—the purest, the greatest, the deepest, and the highest love there is.

Shamballa, Shamballa, Shamballa!
Supreme spiritual realm of infinite divine wisdom, infinite divine love, and infinite divine light.

Shamballa

77 77 77 00 11

triple purifying,
healing, and empowering
shower of life-force energy,
light, and love

Contents

A Brief History of
the Golden Codes of
Shamballa

During the summer of 2006, I was on the island of Milos, a most beautiful Greek island in the Aegean Sea known for its brilliant white rocks and golden sand beaches; its crystal-clear, blue-turquoise waters; and the world-famous statue of Aphrodite of Milos. The island has a long history, and its volcanic origins have provided it with remarkable geodynamic subsoil, rich in a great number of valuable minerals. All of these traits, along with the island's immense natural beauty, create a most-high and powerful resonance energy field on the island and around it.

I was studying esoteric philosophy, meditating intensely and daily, and practicing energy healing techniques, such as Reiki. During this long summer spiritual retreat, I asked inwardly to receive a new energy system for self-cleansing, self-healing, self-empowerment, and self-balancing. I asked for a new and complete energy system of holistic healing, of the highest energy I could receive, with positive effects and benefits on all levels and all areas of life. To my surprise, this system came to me in an unexpected form: it was a mathematical, numerical form. The Golden Codes of Shamballa were received and written down in a single warm, ecstatic afternoon.

Right away, the study and application of the Golden Codes of Shamballa proved greatly helpful and beneficial for me. The codes were uplifting on all levels of myself and in all areas of my life. A year later, in 2007, I was guided to share this wonderful spiritual tool and amazing gift through experiential workshops and also through a small book. I was directed to share it with all the beloved people who wished to positively transform their lives, grow, advance, and evolve to higher and more enlightened states of being.

Since then, a great number of people have been acquainted with the Golden Codes of Shamballa, and I have heard many accounts of positive experiences and received many messages of gratitude. People describe bigger and smaller miracles that often had a life-changing impact. What a manifestation of the mathematically perfect beauty, value, and power of the golden codes! If codes of light, healing, love, and spirit really do exist, then the Golden Codes of Shamballa are definitely to be included among them! And they do—they really do exist, and you, as so many other beloved friends, have discovered them!

From my core, from my heart and soul, I wish for each and every one of you to immediately, directly, and personally perceive, feel, and experience all the wonderful, exquisite, and supreme energies that the golden, fiery, and radiant as the sun codes of light, codes of the great spiritual masters and of Shamballa can bring forth, create, and manifest!

With oceanic and celestial love,
Geom!*
Georgios Mylonas

Introduction

You are about to encounter and receive an innovative and truly amazing system of holistic, energetic, and spiritual healing. This therapeutic system offers purification and protection, wholeness and empowerment, upliftment and guidance, bliss and joy, serenity and freedom. The Golden Codes of Shamballa can be used as potent tools to receive answers to your questions and manifest happiness in your daily life.

This energy system consists of 153 numerical codes of pure light, love, and spirit. They were manifested and generously offered by the infinite, eternal, almighty, and omnibenevolent dimension of spirit, Shamballa. Shamballa is the ethereal crystal residence of the great teachers and the holy archangels of light—the divine spirit beings of the highest wisdom, compassion, beauty, and primordial perfection. The holy archangels of light and the great ascended masters of Shamballa devote themselves to supporting humanity in realizing its potential.

And now, with celestial wisdom and heavenly love, they bless us once more with the Golden Codes of Shamballa.

The Golden Codes of Shamballa are utterly and absolutely positive in nature. They are of the highest and purest light, possessing true spiritual properties and qualities. Their immediate effectiveness and transformative nature—their cleansing, healing, and empowering potential in all areas of human life—are manifested in various ways to the ones who practice them in their daily lives. Each person who applies the Golden Codes of Shamballa in total awareness with the greatest gratitude, respect, care, humility, love, faith, and intention will enjoy all the powerful spiritual energies and the loving divine blessings of the holy archangels of light and the great teachers of Shamballa.

The codes can be applied as often as you wish, and you may experiment freely with them. The use of the codes is completely safe and harmless. You may empower yourself, your loved ones, and all of humanity with an abundance of life-force energy; brilliant spiritual light; and pure, unconditional love—love, the only power that may heal every disease and that can bring everything the mind, the heart, the spirit, and the body—the totality of a human being—wants, needs, and longs for.

What Are the Golden Codes of Shamballa?

* Transcendental, energetically activated, spiritually attuned, and multidimensional codes of light.

* Coded spiritual knowledge, coded focused intention, coded creative power, and coded cellular healing energy.

* Numerical codices; special and specific mathematical forms that permeate all levels of human consciousness.

* A numerical energy healing system that contributes to the manifestation of the wholeness, the divinity, and the infinite possibilities of the human spirit.

* A simple and yet esoterically advanced and highly evolved spiritual technology.

* Numerical codices; sequences of numbers with spiritual value, meaning, and qualities.

*   Amazing numerical spiritual forms; truly precious "spiritual vitamins!"

*   Higher consciousness keys that activate different aspects of the universal cosmic energy, the spirit, and the creative cosmic mind.

*   Sequences of numbers that are dedicated to the benefit of humanity; numerical codes that were created, attuned, and energized by the unseen, positive, and luminous aspect of existence: Shamballa, the ascended masters, teachers, and saints and the holy archangels of light.

*   An easy-to-use, immediately effective system that directs and manifests one's intention to the outer world, everyday life, and material reality.

*   Sequences of numbers that enhance, boost, and uplift one's energy level and level of consciousness.

*   Sequences of numbers that balance and rejuvenate the person holistically on all levels of existence: physical, cellular, etheric, emotional, mental, and spiritual.

*   Sequences of numbers that radiate the vibrations of love (the highest and purest energy of the cosmos) and, therefore, restore the state of purity and vitality.

*   Sequences of numbers that awaken and reactivate the mind, the emotions, and the physical body, its cells, organs, and energy systems.

* A spiritual series of numbers that manifest new, more advanced, and enlightened aspects of the infinite spirit of the world—the spiritual side of reality, which is all powerful and limitless.

* A spiritual series of numbers attuning us to our deepest and highest level of being.

* Illuminating codes that multiply the intention and vibration of love and light on earth and actively contribute to the highest good of all.

* Codes of light that promote spiritual wholeness, fulfillment, health, harmony, balance, bliss, vitality, serenity, and peace.

* Codes of light that work similarly to energetic-spiritual symbols (e.g., the Reiki symbols), mantras (sacred spiritual sounds, words, or affirmations), and invocations.

* A most-ancient but, at the same time, timeless and everlasting spiritual knowledge given in a new way—for the here and now of humanity. For the here and now, now and here!

* A communion of numbers and spirit: a communion of the absolute, objective truth of material/physical reality (numbers) and the absolute, objective truth of all of reality (spirit).

* An effective, simple, practical, and easy-to-use means to balance the two aspects of the mind, logic and intuition, through the parallel invocation of coded serial numbers on

the one hand and spiritual energies, qualities, and powers on the other.

*   A new holistic spiritual technology for the upcoming evolutionary steps of consciousness on earth.

*A gift to humanity!

*   An effective, simple, practical, and easy-to-use way to activate the light body (spiritual body) and increase the physical body's ability to contain and hold more light (life-force energy, etheric vitality).

*   An effective, simple, practical, and easy-to-use means of connecting with the highest reality, no matter how we perceive and name it: God, the divine, the source, the unknown, the spirit soul of the cosmos/world, or the ultimate, transcendental, absolute, supreme, total reality.

*   An empowering means to reach spiritual wholeness, fulfillment, and happiness since the codes upgrade one's spiritual intelligence and, therefore, all other intelligences (e.g., abilities) that a person possesses: mental, emotional, energetic, social, interpersonal, working, technical, scientific, artistic, creative, healing, sexual, bodily, male, female, inner child, and so on.

*   A spiritual science for the new age and for the new humanity—the humanity of freedom, love, and enlightenment; the humanity of harmony, peace, and balance; the humanity of wholeness, oneness, and blissfulness; the

humanity of respect, gratitude, and peace; the humanity of essence, meaning, and purpose; and the spiritual, prosperous, wise, kind, compassionate, aware, and conscious humanity.

Shamballa: Spiritual Dimension of the Ascended Masters and Teachers

Shamballa is a higher dimension of reality and a spiritual dimension. It is a heavenly realm, or, more accurately, it is *the* heavenly realm. It is the divine realm of spiritual light. It is a magnificent and exquisite realm of infinite spiritual light and more real than anything a human being can imagine, think, or perceive from an earthly/material/physical perspective. It is found on a higher, more pure, more luminous, and brighter level of reality. In its brilliant wisdom and love, Shamballa oversees and guides the totality of humanity's spirituality, progressively advancing and evolving all consciousness on our planet. It is the spiritual retreat of the ascended masters, also known as the Great White Brotherhood (representing and expressing the white light, i.e. all colors, energies, and qualities of life and spirit) or the Great Brotherhood of Light.

It is a spiritual hierarchy of saints, teachers, and cosmic beings of the greatest and highest consciousness, wisdom, and love who have ascended to the next evolutionary stage toward divine reality. These older and wiser brothers and sisters serve as humanity's spiritual guardians. They have experienced earthly life in its totality, rising to very high levels of understanding, knowledge, compassion, wisdom, love, and power, which propelled them to transcend the earthly realm. However, they do not completely merge with the infinite absolute divine nirvana and oneness (theosis) as they want to help and guide human beings found on a lower evolutionary stage of consciousness, lost in the turmoil and challenges of earthly life. The ascended masters of the Great Brotherhood of Light lovingly and gently guide us from their ethereal spiritual realm, the dimension of pure light—their home, Shamballa.

Shamballa is the sublimely illuminated crystal city of divine harmony and pure, unconditional love. The teachings of the ascended masters can be summarized as "awareness and love in every single moment and in every single thing." They encompass love and awareness at all times and in all places. Shamballa has offered and sent an abundance of spiritual gifts to humanity.

Among these gifts is this system, the Golden Codes of Shamballa, a set of spiritual, numerical golden codes of light for the building of the new light body and the manifestation of the new life of harmony, oneness, and love. This gift is for every person who deeply desires to experience this new light body and a new life of harmony, oneness, and love, right here and now, in this lifetime! In addition, the Golden Codes of Shamballa bring daily upliftment and, at the same time, a perfect grounding of our spirituality, our spiritual essence, and our higher potential in all areas of life.

Most people would define this kind of an uplifted yet grounded daily life as "happiness," a joyful state of fulfillment that is truly achievable—a state that all of the ascended masters, as well as many human beings right here on earth that have reached the enlightened consciousness, experience daily. They experience this conscious, enlightened state of happiness in each moment. Now, therefore, always and eternally!

Ancient Knowledge in
a Modern Form

The Golden Codes of Shamballa are specific numerical "essences" that awaken and activate different aspects of our all-wise, all-loving, and all-powerful spirit and of our higher and highest self. They are rays of Shamballa, of the light, wisdom, love, and power of all the great teachers, masters, guides, and saints of humanity.

The Golden Codes of Shamballa are sublime and complete; they can even be perceived as sacred since they support and promote the highest good of all: the inner and outer healing of human life and of the entire planet. They correspond with the totality of human experience: the complete spectrum of life on earth. There are specific, spiritual number codes for cleansing, purification, and detoxification; for empowerment and protection; and for increasing love, joy, peace, and serenity in one's life. For the advancement and heightening of consciousness, the enhancement and boost of spiritual evolution and one's psychic and intuitive abilities. There are codes for grounding, inspiration, and creativity; for abundance and prosperity; for blessing and healing; and for the release of negativity and its transmutation. There are also number codes for receiving guidance and healing for a great number of life's conditions, situations, and issues.

The wisdom that created, energized, attuned, and activated the codes is infinite, infinitely life-giving, and wondrous. The love that the codes emanate and radiate is absolute, absolutely mathematical perfect, supreme, and unconditional love. Moreover, the power, the effectiveness, of the codes is evident in their everyday application: consciousness is elevated and expanded, the revitalizing life-force energy flows with ease and abundance, and we are released and set free. We move forward and upward; we are able to get a glimpse of a broader, higher reality. Life is transformed. It takes a complete 360-degree turn toward the light, which shines brightly anew with all new capabilities and potential—capabilities and potential long forgotten or previously not manifested and unexpressed.

The Golden Codes of Shamballa were inspired and created by the ascended teachers of Shamballa—having in mind the current needs and the contemporary world situation—as a path to happiness and enlightenment for the modern light workers and mystics of the planet. The codes were then activated, attuned, and energized by the archangels, who were the holy creators of all the elements of nature and the world and the divine creators of numbers and mathematical laws that permeate, characterize, and construe the cosmos. This esoteric work was completed, grounded, manifested, and shared in order to offer a new way of happiness for the human essence, spirit, and soul: love, joy, freedom, wholeness, fulfillment, oneness, balance, peace, creativity, meaning, purpose, and so on.

May the Golden Codes of Shamballa inspire and bestow blissful joy and joyful bliss on you and all the people around you—joyful bliss and blissful joy to the whole of humanity!

The Golden Codes of Shamballa: Why They Work and Their Benefits

Primarily, the Golden Codes of Shamballa focus the mind. The mind possesses immense known and unknown abilities, potential, and powers. The codes mobilize the spiritual aspect of our own self—our very own spiritual power, which is connected (on an unconscious and super conscious level) with the infinite and supreme divine power, mind, and spirit.

The Golden Codes of Shamballa are guided by the ascended teachers, who designed them, and by a group of archangels of light, whose work is divine mathematics, which is the manifestation of the divine powers through numbers. The codes align and attune the person with the divine mathematics and therefore with universal truth, as numbers and mathematics are objective, universal, and cosmic. The Golden Codes of Shamballa manifest the hidden inner spiritual qualities of numbers, which are contained in all existence—in every single thing.

The Golden Codes of Shamballa attune logic and objective truth with the other aspects of the self: intuition, imagination, emotions, inspiration, and creativity. The union of male and female, of the right and left parts of the brain, of the transcendental and material realms, of heaven and earth, of spirituality and mathematics, and of vital etheric energy and numbers generates a new kind of power!

Energy + Numbers = the Golden Codes of Shamballa = Light

How to Use the Golden Codes of Shamballa

It is best not to use other numbers, numerical series, or codes from other systems while using the Golden Codes of Shamballa. On an esoteric level, the Golden Codes of Shamballa include all other codes, all numerical series, and also all numbers with spiritual energy, power, and potential. They are meant to be used as a whole system, self-sufficient and complete in itself. If you positively, wholeheartedly dedicate yourself to the golden codes with faith, trust, love, respect, and gratitude, having a natural curiosity for them, the one you had for every single thing when you were a child, they will offer abundantly their innumerable gifts.

The focus and intention, along with the love and trust of every individual, play an important role for the activation of the codes. When you give 100 percent of your faith, your intention, and your love to a system as a method for daily spiritual illumination, upliftment, and happiness, the system will reward you. You will reap the fruits of your efforts. What you give, you get—never something less. Ask and you shall receive, and, at the same time, give and you shall receive!

Do not modify or alter the codes. Part of the beneficial energy and wise power that the codes hold rises from their repeated (the energy connection of the person with the codes strengthens through daily repetition), unchanging, and focused application, as well as from the collective use and the total intention, focus, and energy of all the people lovingly activating them on a daily basis.

How to Start with the Golden Codes of Shamballa

Read the Golden Codes of Shamballa from the beginning to the end in the order they are given.

Reading the totality of the codes in their original succession activates them in such a way that they become awakened, grounded, and coded in your energy, which includes your aura, your mind, your spirit, and your subconscious. The activation of the codes expands you to multiple states of consciousness. People often feel rejuvenated as they read the codes, or they experience light, love, peace, serenity, joy, or an astounding spiritual field. At times, people speak of experiencing a state of trance, overexcitement, or bliss. Signs of cleansing might be also present, such as yawning or sneezing, hotness or coldness, tears, dizziness, tiredness, and a variety of other "peculiar" reactions. All reactions are considered natural, welcomed, and expected. The codes are being activated within your energy field. They start to work!

After your first initial reading, you can proceed to a second one and a third one. It takes about twenty minutes to read aloud all the codes in a slow, meditative pace. Set aside a few minutes of relaxation to feel the energies after you finish reading the codes. It is advised to start by reading the codes in their entirety and original succession aloud, in a slow and meditative pace, at least once or twice a day for a week and then to proceed to work with the individual codes.

Collectively, the codes are transcendental and complete in the way they work as a holistic care and support for your aura, mind, body, and spirit. The entirety of the codes cleanses, heals, empowers, and balances every part of your being—all energies and qualities within and around you.

After reading the codes in their entirety daily for one week, you may feel like choosing one, two, or more codes to work on specific areas and situations in a variety of ways. Use the codes intuitively, either individually or in various combinations. Remember that the codes can do no harm and you can do no wrong since mathematics is an objective truth and reality of the universe. Furthermore, divine mathematics, numbers that are enhanced with energetic and spiritual qualities, awaken exciting new aspects and possibilities of the all-wise and almighty divine spirit of love and happiness that is embodied and represented by all the ascended masters and the holy archangels of Shamballa, the divine dimension of infinite light and love.

How to Apply the Golden Codes of Shamballa

During the first week, read the Golden Codes of Shamballa in their entirety. Read them in the given succession, slowly and meditatively, in a relaxed state of mind. You may repeat the codes silently or aloud to enhance their effectiveness through the vibrational power of spoken word. Read them at least once a day to activate your spiritual essence and to connect with the codes on all levels. The totality of the golden codes is truly powerful. Prepare yourself for positive change! Welcome positive energies, positive qualities, and positive attributes to your life. Claim your spiritual rights: love, joy, good fortune, prosperity, abundance, harmony, balance, peace, serenity, health, power, knowledge, wholeness, unity, bliss, and happiness! Claim your rights! Claim your spiritual rights, and then just accept them. Claim and accept!

Over the following days, concentrate on a situation or an issue that preoccupies you. Read the totality of the golden codes, or choose a specific code that you intuitively believe will help you. Repeat the code or codes to receive guidance for your issue. Engage in this process for a few days.

When reading the golden codes, you read and recite everything: first the word *Shamballa*, then the numbers, and then the energy, function, or quality that the code evokes. For example, you can say, "Shamballa twelve-twelve, supremacy of spirit" so as to claim and evoke the supremacy of spirit over all things. You can say, "Shamballa seven-seven-seven-seven, shower of love" so as to call forth the pure energy of unconditional love. You can say, "Shamballa four, grounding" to ground and connect yourself to Mother Earth.

Read and recite the numbers of each code as you perceive them. As an example, you may say "Shamballa twelve-twelve, supremacy of spirit" or "Shamballa one-two, one-two, supremacy of spirit." Either way is effective. Read what you perceive at each moment.

When reading the entirety of the codes, read each code only once. When working with individual codes, you may read them and recite each one three times or more. After you repeat a code three times (or as many times as you feel like), pause for a while and notice the energy: the way you feel, what you sense, and what happens inside or around you. Notice everything very carefully. Become an extremely good observer of everything! You may keep your eyes gently closed and open them again once you are ready to proceed to the reading of the next code.

Choose your favorite code—the one that attracts you the most—and think about it. Evoke it either mentally or aloud over and over again during the day. You can also whisper, chant, or sing the codes. Write down the golden codes of your choice on paper. Use a variety of colors. Experiment! Place your favorite codes everywhere. Experiment, observe, and experiment again!

You may also energetically cleanse and charge your water and your food by placing a paper with a code written on it underneath it. You may recite the code silently or audibly before eating food or drinking water. By reciting the golden codes out loud, you can energetically cleanse your house, your workplace, or any other area. Use the codes generously, freely, and fearlessly with love, faith, respect, awareness, joy, and gratitude.

The Golden Codes of Shamballa were created and shared in order to offer the energies of happiness and everything that is necessary for its daily manifestation— our complete potential. And this is exactly what we truly wish to you, from within our heart, spirit, and soul.

In mathematically absolute, supreme, and infinite love,
Shamballa and its teachers

Questions and Answers

Why are the codes "golden"?
First, "golden" refers to the value of the codes. They are as valuable as pure gold.

Second, the codes are often seen or sensed clairvoyantly as golden numbers, radiating and emanating golden light—the light of the source, of the spirit, and of logos (divine consciousness).

Third, the codes represent the brilliant light and the warm luminosity of the sun, which is fiery golden-white and constitutes the highest source of life for the entire planet, all forms of life on earth, and the whole of humanity.

Should I recite the codes silently or out loud? How many times is it necessary to repeat them? Should I recite the word *Shamballa* and the function of the codes as well?
You can recite the codes silently or audibly. It is advised to recite the codes audibly in order to manifest their full potential. The number of repetitions depends entirely on your mood and how far you want to reach. Start by reading

the codes in their entirety and original succession aloud for a week, and then proceed in working with the individual codes. If you are working with a certain code, you may repeat it many times with a slow, meditative pace, pausing and sensing the energy. You first recite the word *Shamballa*, then the number, and, at the end, the function of the code.

How do I properly recite the numbers, for example "7777" or "4343"?

You recite the numbers as you perceive them at that moment. For example, 7777 is "seven-seven-seven-seven" or "seventy-seven, seventy-seven" and 4343 is "four-three-four-three" or "forty-three, forty-three."

Is it possible to do harm instead of good by using the codes improperly?

No, absolutely not! Do not worry about that—not for one moment! The codes have been created, guided, and shared by infinite wisdom and love. No harm may arise from the golden codes; they have absolutely pure and positive vibrations. The codes serve the light, they offer light, they originate from the light, and they lead to the light. In fact, they *are* light in the form of numbers! They are a unique activation and manifestation of the light, the universal spiritual energy. The codes have been created by the great teachers with the help of angelic beings in a time where there is a vast shift in human consciousness and new spiritual methods and technologies are being developed. A new way of being is leading us to the most advanced levels of spiritual awareness yet known. Humanity is ready for awakening, and this will be achieved in various ways. This spiritual technology of numerical codes of light is one of these ways.

How do I know that the codes derive from Shamballa and the ascended masters and not from somewhere else?
You may simply take a leap of faith and trust the wisdom, the power, and the energy, the love, the healing effects, and the benefits of the numbers. Numbers are truth; numbers, by themselves and on their own, are truly divine codes of creation! Turn to your heart center in order to find an answer to this question, thereby attuning more with your own spiritual intuition and inner guidance. The answer will surface. You and you alone can decide what is right for you and what path of awareness you are to follow, for you are a unique and whole spiritual being. The Golden Codes of Shamballa—and actually all numbers—entirely belong and are attuned to the light of creation.

What happens if I don't like a certain code?
That may signify that there is some blockage, either on an energetic-etheric or on a mental or emotional level, of the function or quality that the individual code represents. You may proceed with other codes till you resolve or unblock your issues regarding the particular topic. Alternatively, you may work for a short time with the code with which

you feel strange or foreign until you feel unblocked and reach awareness. Follow your intuition.

Why am I drawn to certain codes more than others?
Most likely, those certain codes awaken inside you memories of perfection, memories of the era when we were one: one with the whole, one with perfection, and one with the heavens in perfect harmony, when we were one with the One in everlasting, divine, unconditional, blissful happiness. The codes remind you of your higher potential and your divine nature and blueprint. The codes guide and assist you in returning to your divine essence—your true self. As you overcome specific problems, you become the master of your life, and you attract more peace, bliss, spiritual light, and love. Open your heart—your renewed, clean, pure, freed, and brilliantly, radiantly enlightened golden heart.

After using the codes, I have intense dreams or some coincidences happen in my life. How is that possible?
The codes purify, renew, and rejuvenate our body's energy system since they replenish the body with greater amounts of vital life-force etheric energy. You positively change from the inside out. Part of this healing process is to break through the veils of illusion and unawareness and to release past memories of pain and suffering that keep you tied to the wheel of karma. This transformation may evoke peculiar dreams or even visions, states of awareness, memories, strange coincidences, and increased synchronicity. Observe and embrace your new experiences;

welcome them warmly. Open your mind widely as you widely opened your heart—your renewed, clean, pure, freed, and brilliantly, radiantly enlightened golden mind.

Can I use the codes to heal a physical health issue?

The codes unfold our inner peace and harmony, enhance our emotional and mental clarity, replenish us with positive energy and light, and rejuvenate and uplift us. All those elements are vital for good emotional and physical health and well-being. Nevertheless, the practice of the golden codes does not replace formal medical or mental diagnosis and treatment. It is advised to consult a medical expert for any health issues. Please be respectful of the codes and their practice and never promise to heal other people. The practice of the codes is a spiritual journey of positive transformation that is unique for each person.

I don't understand certain codes. For example, what is the meaning of the code "Shamballa 606 Autumn"?

That is one of the wonderful things about the codes. They do not exclusively address our rational, conscious mind. They function on a broad spectrum and on multiple levels of consciousness. At a relaxed, meditative moment of inner peace and calmness, you may inwardly ask yourself, *What can this code mean? Where does it help me?* Imagine possible answers and explanations. Be open to receive. Keep in mind that not all codes can be explained or rationalized. It's not even necessary! The unknown, the inexplicable, and the transcendental have their own beauty, value, and purpose!

I noticed identical codes and numbers with different functions, such as "Shamballa 99 00, higher self," "Shamballa 9900, heal the future," and "Shamballa 9900, success, if God wills it." Likewise, different codes and numbers have the same function, such as "Shamballa 99 00, higher self" and "Shamballa 787 88 99, Higher Self." Is there some mistake?

The codes were received in their entirety in a single afternoon through a continuous flow of higher inspiration and ecstatic writing. Afterward, I felt rightful not to modify or correct the repetitions of specific numbers. In all likelihood, Shamballa and its teachers wish to give prominence to the specific numbers and their functions and qualities. It's also possible that the same number embodies various energies and qualities or that we can express the same action in several ways: "higher self," "success, if God wills it," and "heal the future." Those are concepts of an interconnected nature that complement each other. As for the two codes related to the higher self, I feel that they manifest a connection with our higher self at different levels of our existence.

Can I combine the codes with prayer or meditation? Can I combine the codes with Reiki or other energy healing systems?

Absolutely! You can choose your favorite codes or the codes you feel that correspond with a certain issue and repeat them before and after your prayer. You can apply the same procedure for meditation, Reiki, and any other energy healing system. By reciting the codes before and after your daily rituals, your prayer becomes more alive and conscious, your meditation becomes deeper and more intense, Reiki becomes more empowering and rejuvenating, and every other energy healing and spiritual method is illuminated and enhanced as its higher qualities come forth. Feel free to experiment, and feel freely!

I noticed that there are references to God and other spiritual figures like angels. Do I need to be a Christian or to believe in God in order to benefit from the codes?

It is not a prerequisite to believe in the existence of spiritual beings, but it is extremely helpful to keep your mind, heart, and spirit open—wide open to new possibilities and other states and levels of life, consciousness, and reality. Life is an ever-expanding, ever-continuous, ever-changing, evolving, and unfolding process. Keep your mind, your spirit, and your heart clean, light, and open as a child's, and you will not find yourself blocked or stuck in this process. You will be able to go with the flow of life. This is the essence and the definition of being truly happy and blissful.

Are the codes contradictory to religion? Do the codes comprise a religious system of their own?

Absolutely not! The codes are of a completely and totally positive nature, full of love and light. As such, they don't contradict any religion. It is a numerical set with spiritual healing aspects. A system, in order to be considered a religion, needs to be comprised of various elements, such as dogma, philosophy, morals, structure, leadership, hierarchy, rituals, and so on. The codes are not related to such elements, so they cannot even be compared with religious systems. They are compatible with every religion. More precisely, they are compatible with each and every individual human being, religious or not!

Are the codes associated with magic?

Magic has been often connected to negative and low vibrational situations, energies, teachings, and systems. The codes are in no way connected with these. The numerical codices exclusively belong to the light. Numbers are reality, and reality is light. Therefore, numbers are light.

How is it possible that simple numbers can bring about positive change and activate energies, qualities, strengths, virtues, and so on?

The numerical codes and numerical sequences function as symbols. Numbers permeate everything. All things can be (or can be in the future) measured or explained with numbers. It is an objective, stable, specific, and precise way of measuring reality. When we evoke specific numerical codices, we also evoke distinguishing qualities of the infinite reality. Additionally, the Golden Codes of Shamballa are energetically attuned to the highest spiritual forces. This attunement has been facilitated by spiritual beings of a higher consciousness (the ascended masters) and creative universal and cosmic forces (the archangels). By meditating and focusing on these numbers while having specific healing intentions in mind, we align ourselves with our higher soul qualities and also with these superior, spiritual, and sublime beings of light. This alignment is actually a process of unification, and unity is wholeness, totality, and completion—vital ingredients for happiness.

Are the golden codes related to Shamballa Reiki?

Shamballa Reiki was developed in the 90s by a wonderful teacher, John Armitage, also known as Hari Baba. It is considered an expanded version of Reiki; energy healing from the perspective of Shamballa and the ascended teachers. Compared to traditional Usui Reiki, Shamballa Reiki teaches different concepts and techniques and it offers a great number of meditations, channelings as well as spiritual information. It was also named Shamballa Multidimensional Healing System and it was later renamed into New Paradigm Multidimensional Transformation. Being already an Usui Reiki Teacher, I received the Shamballa Reiki training, which greatly empowered my connection to Shamballa and the ascended masters. Although there is a similar concept in Shamballa Reiki, a few numbers that act as energy codes, the Golden Codes of Shamballa, as an entire and complete system on its own, came separately, independently and unexpectedly, a few years later. Nevertheless, it would not be possible without my prior experiences with Shamballa Reiki and I would like to express my deepest gratitude to all of my teachers and especially to John Armitage for his most precious and valuable teachings.

Are there more codes available?

The golden codes that are given in this book constitute a complete system. There is no need for additional codes. The existing numbers cover a totality of experiences and circumstances. However, there are certain additional codes that are given for personal use during a workshop on the Shamballa Codes. They are personal codes and are different for each individual. They are used for further energetic and spiritual development, advancement, and evolution. Online workshops are available at *www. energiesoflight.com* and *www.universityofreiki.com*.

Can I use the codes on behalf of another person? If so, how?

You may use the healing energies and properties of the codes on behalf of another person as long as you ask the person for permission. You must have the person's informed consent. You must always respect the freedom of will of each person; it is divine law. In case you cannot reach the person (for instance, the person is in a coma), you can request permission in a state of meditation from the person's higher self—his or her eternal and wise spirit. Proceed to declare that you only wish for the highest good of the person and you have no intention of interfering with his or her choices and free will. Finally, declare that you act with awareness of absolute freedom and out of pure, unconditional love. State the name of the person three times at the beginning of the session, and you may think of him or her as you recite the codes. At the end, lovingly thank the person and send (visualize the person in the energy of) love, light, and vital life-force energy.

When I am reciting the codes, I feel euphoria or/and agitation, and afterward, I feel like I am in a trance. What is happening?

As we recite the codes, our inner essence and our highest nature are being awakened and activated. Our core is emanating spiritual energy/light. Our energy system is filled with an abundant flow of pure, vital energy. We overflow with serenity, joy, and love. Our consciousness expands, we see things crystal clear, and our mind experiences its spiritual nature and its divine origins. The codes lead directly to states that human consciousness can achieve only through prolonged and deep meditation.

While I recite the codes, I get a headache and a sense of burning fever. Is that normal?

Yes, it's normal. The Golden Codes of Shamballa detox, purify, and rejuvenate our energy system and therefore all levels of self. This process may cause unpleasant sensations or symptoms that will soon disappear.

While I recite the codes, I experience a cold air flow or intense heat. What does this mean?

What you feel is the energy of Shamballa: the energy of pure spirit and of the great spiritual masters. Observe, experience, and enjoy it to the fullest extent!

While I was reciting the codes, someone interrupted me. Should I start over from the beginning?
You don't need to start from the beginning; just continue where you left off.

Do I need to have faith in the codes in order for them to be effective?
No. Their action has been observed even when you simply recite them out of curiosity or experimentally or mechanically. The energy codes are transcendental just like numbers are; they exist and vibrate independently from us, as strange and otherworldly as this may seem!

Can the codes replace other self-development processes, energy healing methods, and spiritual systems?
The codes cannot replace other spiritual processes or self-development methods, but they complement and enhance them. The codes are a unique and complete system of spiritual expansion for everyone. They are mathematically precise, accurate, and true!

Do the codes stimulate cleansing and purification just like Reiki or other energy healing systems?
The codes may often bring about cleansing and purification just as other healing energy systems. Purification is a natural and necessary result but positive and beneficial in essence. The duration of purification varies from hours to a few months, its intensity varies from soft to

profound, and its kind (physical, energetic, emotional, mental, spiritual, and so on) is different for every individual. As we go through a purification period, it's essential to take good, loving care of ourselves with proper natural diet, balanced exercise, contact with nature, walks outside to ground ourselves, relaxing baths and showers, plenty of mineral water, adequate sleeping, meditation and conscious/positive thinking and speaking, awareness, responsible choices, and enjoyment of loving, caring, deep, meaningful, and harmonious contact with loved ones.

Are there any codes specifically for children, animals, and plants? Are they safe to use?

Yes, there are golden codes specially intended for children, animals, and plants. They are designed to be mild and yet precise and effective. You will encounter them while you read the codes in their totality. They can be used exclusively for energy work with children, animals, and plants.

Can I communicate with angels, archangels, and/or with my higher self by using the codes?

Yes! There are corresponding codices through which you may receive the energies and qualities and also connect and communicate with these heavenly beings of light and pure spirit. The benefit of this pure, angelic communion is nourishment for your soul!

Who are Metatron, Mahatma, and Melchizedek?

All three beings are found in texts of esoteric spiritual traditions, and they were encountered by great mystics and sages of humanity to verify their existence and beneficence.

Metatron is said to be one of the highest archangels in heaven and to sit right next to God's throne. He brings enlightenment and the gift of ascension to human beings. Enoch became Archangel Metatron once he ascended to heaven.

Mahatma means "great soul" *(maha atma)* and refers to any higher/ascended teacher of the light. The Mahatma energy is the energy of the soul, the energy of the "I Am Presence", and the energy of the divine source, with which all the great spiritual teachers of humanity were in perfect alignment and attunement.

Melchizedek is the sacred name of the Cosmos and the spiritual name of the universe. It is the consciousness and spiritual essence of the universe. The greatest teachers were initiated into this energy, also known as the order of Melchizedek.

All three beings bestow utterly and totally positive energies as they are masters and spiritual beings of the purest and the highest light. Their loving, healing energies uplift us into higher states of spiritual love, wisdom, and power. They bring us closer to the Divine since they themselves are the closest to the divine known beings, intelligences, and powers.

Is there a meditation I can do when working with the codes?

Just sit comfortably with your spine straight, and gently close your eyes.

Take ten slow and deep breaths. Breathe in through the nose, and breathe out through the mouth. In your mind, count your breaths. Count ten deep and slow breaths. Conscious, energetic, and life- and light-giving breaths. Do it with your full attention and in full awareness. With each exhalation, you release negativity and all that you no longer need, and with each inhalation, you receive and are filled with pure positivity, life, and light. Inhale light, life, and positivity; exhale everything you want to let go of. Ten deep, conscious, energetic, and life- and light-giving breaths...

Then, relax. Ask your body to relax and feel it gradually do so more and more. It becomes soft. Ask your mind to relax and feel that it is happening. Your mind lets go. It lets go of every tension; it lets go of all tensions. Your mind is becoming calm and still, like a beautiful, quiet lake, mirroring the clear blue sky. Wish peace and serenity to your body and to your mind.

In this relaxed, peaceful, and serene state, imagine a bright white light showering you. It comes from above, from a great height, from the highest top, the highest point in existence. Imagine it. Visualize it. See it. Feel it. Or just think about it.

White light is showering you, cleansing you, and filling you. Feel its wonderful warmth and radiant luminosity waving through you, eliminating darkness, bringing vitality and joy to all of your organs, and bringing illumination, love, and life to every cell of your being.

Feel the light. Feel it more and more—brighter and brighter, clean and pure, vital and healing. Relax into it; let it flow abundantly everywhere. Let life and light flow to all parts of your body, to every system, to every organ, and to every cell. Let life and light flow to all systems, to all organs, and to all cells. Let life and light flow through your whole body. It is being deeply rejuvenated; it is being completely restored.

Perfect health, perfect well-being, perfect balance, and perfect harmony are being achieved. See and feel your body filled with radiant life-light, being a unity of clear and bright life-light. You are manifesting perfect, absolute, and total health, well-being, balance, and harmony.

Stay for a few moments in this higher state, a state of complete, total, and perfect life and light.

Now, feel a flame in the center of your chest. It is being awakened. Observe this golden flame. "Divine wisdom... divine power...divine love." Think and feel these words, and let the golden flame expand and radiate through you and around you. Bless your home, your family, your city, the planet, all human beings, all beings, and Mother

Earth. Bless them with loving kindness and this divine, golden, loving light—the golden light of love. From your heart and your soul, wish them all the best, their greatest and highest good. Powerfully affirm it.

Stay for a few moments in this expanded state, a state of complete, total, and perfect love and light.

Feel yourself within your physical body healthy, empowered, and balanced, completely within your body, centered, and grounded. You are peaceful, joyful, and blissful. You are pure, you are clean, and you are radiant. Light, love, and life! Take three full, deep breaths, and open your eyes.

Continue your day in a spiritual, loving, peaceful, joyful, enlightened state, being fully conscious and aware.

You may practice this meditation any time you wish. Practice daily to advance more in your spiritual work and to experience optimal energy healing results. You may apply the meditation and then recite the codes or do the meditation following the recitation of the codes. You may also recite your favorite code or the code you work with as you do the meditation while being in the relaxed, meditative state within the energy of light. Or, you can use this meditation separately and independently of the codes in order to add a positive, beneficial, uplifting, healing meditative practice to your daily life.

Is there any affirmation or invocation I can use?

If you want to use an invocation, please feel free to apply the following:

> *"Beloved divine source,*
> *Shamballa, Shamballa, Shamballa,*
> *Angels and great teachers of the highest light,*
> *I call upon you!*
> *Please purify, purify, purify me,*
> *cleanse, cleanse, cleanse me,*
> *heal, heal, heal me,*
> *illuminate, illuminate, illuminate me,*
> *enlighten, enlighten, enlighten me*
> *on all levels, on all levels, on all levels.*
> *I call forth the infinitely perfect light*
> *of your total, absolute, and supreme wisdom and love!*
> *Infinite light, infinite light, infinite light!*
> *So be it, and so it is! I love you, thank you!"*

You can use this invocation before you start to recite the codes or independently at any time you wish during the day. Repeat it at least three times, slowly and meditatively, with love and gratitude, feeling it deeply from within your heart and soul.

Do I have to use the invocation and the meditation previously given in order to use the codes?

No. Use the codes by themselves; they are meant to be applied on their own. They are complete. Nevertheless, if you feel that you want to meditate or do an invocation, feel free to practice the ones offered previously. They are spiritually uplifting and empowering for all levels of the self!

Can I make different lists of codes that have similar functions or common themes so as to cleanse, heal, and empower different areas of my life?

Yes. Excellent! You can put all the codes concerning abundance and work together, all the codes about love and intimate relationships together, all the physical healing codes together, all the emotional and mental healing codes together, all the angelic codes together, all the cleansing codes together, all the spiritual growth and advancement codes together, and so on. Choose an area you want to work on or an issue that preoccupies you, and list all the related codes. Write them down, and then recite them. Experiment and practice and experiment and practice some more!

Why is it that each page features only one code?

At first, the codes were given to others in the form of notes. When people saw and experienced various benefits, the idea of a book came forth so that more people could receive all of these wonderful energies and gifts. It was clear in my mind that each page would be dedicated to one and only code and that each and every code would be on its own separate and individual page. In this way, the reader may open the book and see, by chance, one code that is an answer to his or her thoughts or that may inspire him or her. Most important, the reader can focus on each code individually. The reader is able to pause and remain on each different page, on each and different code, in order to relax, observe, sense, and feel the energy. This simple, spacious Zen method is best for meditation. Each code's number, function, and vibration is seen and felt so much more directly, clearly, and vividly when it is seen individually on paper. The meditative experience, activation, and absorption of the code's golden light is much greater.

When, how, and why were the golden codes given?
Geom!* (the spiritual name of Georgios Mylonas, from Athens, Greece) was working intensely and for many years with the energies of archangels, studying, practicing, and teaching energy, spiritual, and esoteric healing methods. At some point, he came in contact with the energies of the ascended masters—the energies of Shamballa—and he continued to work equally intensely with them for another extensive period of time. The Golden Codes of Shamballa were given to Geom!* in the summer of 2006, following his request to receive a complete healing system for total energy and spiritual cleansing and purification, advancement and growth, illumination, and enlightenment.

Geom!* asked for an energy healing system that would be immediate and direct, effective, and safe; a system addressed to beloved people of all energy and spiritual levels and backgrounds; and a system that served in a substantial way the greatest good of all of humanity and the life purpose of every individual. He asked for a system that would provide some of the infinite gifts that the divine source offers in its supreme love, compassion, mercy, and grace.

The answer to his heartfelt request came almost right away, and the totality of the golden codes were received in an ecstatic and transcendental way on a single afternoon. The system was a complete numerical system with amazing energy healing benefits, qualities, and attributes. Because of their form, Geom!* originally thought that the codes were intended for a limited number of people that had reached a certain high level of spiritual awareness and growth; however, the continuous guidance of Shamballa was that his original request had really been answered and the codes were to be accessible to all people. This would be achieved by offering and giving everything out through a book and a website. And thus, it happened!

From then on, a great number of beloved people have testified and experienced in their everyday lives the exquisite and wondrous golden energies of the Golden Codes of Shamballa!

The Golden Codes of
Shamballa

Shamballa

12

divine spirit

Shamballa

1212

supremacy of spirit

Shamballa

12121212

divine vibrations, clearing of blockages

Shamballa

991

clear away evil-eye influences

Shamballa

1313

good luck, synchronicity

Shamballa

1010

transcendence, completion

Shamballa

1111

renewal, unification, grounding

Shamballa

4

grounding

Shamballa

44

manifestation

Shamballa

4444

manifestation, materialization

Shamballa

94

divine purpose and divine plan

Shamballa

7774

trust, acceptance, letting go

Shamballa

9994

faith

Shamballa

7373

detoxification,
optimal body weight
and health for men

Shamballa

4343

detoxification,
optimal body weight
and health for women

Shamballa

9990

angelic number, angels of light,
angels of God, angels of love

Shamballa

776654

healing of a problem,
situation, health issue

Shamballa

77

sacred energies

Shamballa

1112

change

Shamballa

1012

upliftment, elevation, dawn

Shamballa

7777

shower of love

Shamballa

88

attraction, love, union, passion

Shamballa

7788

emotional wholeness,
clarity, harmony, healing

Shamballa

8899

mental wholeness,
clarity, harmony, healing

Shamballa

8809

physical wellness

Shamballa

333

joy

Shamballa

96

serenity

Shamballa

99

euphoria, rejuvenation

Shamballa

108

spiritual dedication

Shamballa

109

spiritual evolution

Shamballa

44447

earth healing

Shamballa

444488

world peace

Shamballa

444499

planetary enlightenment,
heaven on earth

GEORGIOS MYLONAS

Shamballa

555

comprehension of a situation

Shamballa

554

learning

Shamballa

559

memory

Shamballa

557

mental balance

Shamballa

101010

karmic lessons,
comprehension

Shamballa

101011

karmic lessons,
energy, light,
transcendence, mercy

Shamballa

101012

karmic lessons, clearing

Shamballa

101077

karmic lessons,
profound healing,
activation, release,
divine energies, freedom

Shamballa

7

blessing

Shamballa

77

multiple blessings

Shamballa

777

multiple blessings
with love and healing

Shamballa

10

salutation

Shamballa

808

spring

Shamballa

707

summer

Shamballa

606

fall

Shamballa

202101

winter

Shamballa

94994

celestial, astrological,
planetary and zodiac
cleansing of negative influences

Shamballa

76767676

harmonization of opposites,
good and bad, yin and yang,
positive and negative

Shamballa

63

healing of the female energy
and female aspect

Shamballa

73

healing of the male energy and male aspect

Shamballa

884

healing of the inner child

Shamballa

1111111111

child healing

Shamballa

222

animal healing

Shamballa

771

plant healing

Shamballa

8801

rejuvenation

Shamballa

7703

beauty

Shamballa

994

abundance

Shamballa

9910

financial independence
and maturity

Shamballa

9912

financial empowerment
and new openings

Shamballa

7771

etheric vitality,
bioenergy, prana, chi,
life-force energy healing

Shamballa

77 78

guardian angel

Shamballa

99 00

higher self

Shamballa

546474

loving kindness

Shamballa

1010 1111 1212

protection on all levels

Shamballa

8

protection SOS

Shamballa

07 21

healing SOS

Shamballa

10

protection

Shamballa

21

goal, aim

Shamballa

0011

heal the past

Shamballa

9900

heal the future

Shamballa

11 12 11

holographic and quantum
healing and clearing

Shamballa

11 11 44 44

relaxation

Shamballa

8989

dreams

Shamballa

000

peaceful sleep

Shamballa

0000

dreams within the light

Shamballa

00000

sleep of the master

Shamballa

11117

spiritual, energetic, mental awakening

Shamballa

4567

emotional upliftment,
recovery from sadness,
negativity, grief, attachment

Shamballa

9900

success, if God wills it

Shamballa

0099

God is creating my life

Shamballa

80

I love God,
I love the light,
I love humanity,
and I love to love.

Shamballa

7878

meditation

Shamballa

1 88 98

nutritional healing

Shamballa

0101

inner divine value,
dignity, humility,
return to innocence

Shamballa

99899

spiritual truth,
overcoming illusions
regardless of the cost

Shamballa

9898

rescue (rescue remedy)

Shamballa

4411

energy empowerment
of a specific organ

Shamballa

4400

energy empowerment
for all body systems

Shamballa

4477

empowerment for
self-healing processes,
instant healing,
inner empowerment

Shamballa

447700

release, purification, regeneration
(to overcome a disease)

Shamballa

4488

multiple-level healing

Shamballa

4949

increased energy flow

Shamballa

48888 9999 7777

healing involving
materialization,
dematerialization,
transmutation,
dense matter

Shamballa

7 801

angels of the highest
first creative light

Shamballa

7 809

angels of meditation,
connection, guidance,
spiritual work, and healing

Shamballa

7 808

angels of love, peace, and joy

Shamballa

7 8000

angels of wholeness,
good fortune,
protection, and happiness

Shamballa

5555

optimal communication

Shamballa

5555 333

communication, peace,
serenity, joy, clarity, patience

Shamballa

448844

independence, rights, strength

Shamballa

449

endurance

Shamballa

774

hope

Shamballa

776655331

forgiveness, release

Shamballa

008800

Shamballa initiation

Shamballa

110011

powerful energies
of the source, the logos, and the spirit
of the creative divine trinity

Shamballa

6600

work,
purpose of life, divine intervention

Shamballa

6611

work,
creativity, wholeness

Shamballa

6677

work,
healing, energizing

Shamballa

6644

work,
success, abundance, victory

Shamballa

6688

work,
peace, harmony and balance

Shamballa

6699

work,
completion, new beginning,
guidance, delegation

Shamballa

3383

empowerment of friendship

Shamballa

3322

empowerment of creativity,
strength, talents,
self-confidence, and self-worth

Shamballa

3377

energetic empowerment,
upliftment, rejuvenation

Shamballa

3366

empowerment of cleansing,
spiritual mysteries, knowledge

Shamballa

3344

empowerment of manifestation,
success, abundance

Shamballa

33 88 99

empowerment of love,
attraction, passion,
personal relationships, companionship

Shamballa

3310

empowerment of body

Shamballa

3312

empowerment of enlightenment
and spirit

Shamballa

3313

empowerment of good fortune,
synchronicity, flow

Shamballa

3388

empowerment of harmony,
serenity, peace, freedom

Shamballa

3393

empowerment of joy and bliss

Shamballa

44 44 4

cellular body regeneration

Shamballa

983

forgiveness of the self
and liberating consciousness
from all kinds of negativity

Shamballa

6655 983

detachment from
dependency and ill habits;
purification of everyday life,
substances, chemicals, and so on

Shamballa

6655 10 11 12 13

energetic protection
from radiation, waves, smoke, pollution,
radioactivity, chemicals, viruses, parasites,
illnesses, electromagnetic-negative fields
and factors of all kinds and of all intensities;
purification of accumulated negativity and
toxicity

Shamballa

787

Archangel Michael

Shamballa

789

Archangel Gabriel

Shamballa

780

Archangel Uriel

Shamballa

787 77

Archangel Raphael

Shamballa

789 99

Archangel Metatron

Shamballa

787 66

Melchizedek

Shamballa

787 88

Mahatma

Shamballa

787 88 99

Higher Self

Shamballa

11 787 88 99 00

I Am Presence, Infinite Source, God

Shamballa

6699 966

answers, messages, channeling

Shamballa

88 0 88

opening for healing

Shamballa

88 10 88

closing for healing, completion

Shamballa

66 77 88

healing of fear and phobias

Shamballa

779900

invocation to the spiritual laws
and the divine rights

Shamballa

77 77 77 00 11

triple purifying, healing, and empowering
shower of life-force energy, light, and love

Shamballa

66 99

balance of the energy centers (chakras)

Shamballa

66 99 11 22 33 44 55 66 77

balance of the energy bodies
and of their elements

Shamballa

00 10

balanced and complete integration
of the Shamballa Golden Codes
within the body, the energy system,
the mind, and the spirit

Shamballa

00 11

deeper grounding
of the Shamballa Golden Codes

Shamballa

00 12

greater manifestation
of the Shamballa Golden Codes
on every level and for every occasion

Shamballa

00 11 11 22

immediate manifestation
of the Shamballa Golden Codes
and of their beneficial effects

Shamballa

00 11 22 33 44 55 66 77

harmonization and alignment
of the person with
the Shamballa Golden Codes
on all levels

Shamballa

OOOOOO

purification, regeneration,
and harmonization of all of
the Shamballa Golden Codes

Shamballa

10 10 10 10

May the highest plan,
the highest good,
and the Divine Will prevail,
Amen. Thank you!

The Golden Codes
of Shamballa, Index

Shamballa 4444 manifestation, materialization

Shamballa 94 divine purpose and divine plan

Shamballa 7774 trust, acceptance, letting go

Shamballa 9994 faith

Shamballa 7373 detoxification, optimal body weight and health for men

Shamballa 4343 detoxification, optimal body weight and health for women

Shamballa 9990 angelic number, angels of light, angels of God, angels of love

Shamballa 776654 healing of a problem, situation, health issue

Shamballa 77 sacred energies

Shamballa 1112 change

Shamballa 1012 upliftment, elevation, dawn

Shamballa 7777 shower of love

Shamballa 88 attraction, love, union, passion

Shamballa 7788 emotional wholeness, clarity, harmony, healing

Shamballa 8899 mental wholeness, clarity, harmony, healing

Shamballa 8809 physical wellness

Shamballa 333 joy

Shamballa 96 serenity

Shamballa 99 euphoria, rejuvenation

Shamballa 108 spiritual dedication

Shamballa 109 spiritual evolution

Shamballa 44447 earth healing

Shamballa 444488 world peace

Shamballa 444499 planetary enlightenment, heaven on earth

Shamballa 555 comprehension of a situation

Shamballa 554 learning

Shamballa 559 memory

Shamballa 557 mental balance

Shamballa 101010 karmic lessons, comprehension

Shamballa 101011 karmic lessons, energy, light, transcendence, mercy

Shamballa 101012 karmic lessons, clearing

Shamballa 101077 karmic lessons, profound healing, activation, release, divine energies, freedom

Shamballa 7 blessing

Shamballa 77 multiple blessings

Shamballa 777 multiple blessings with love and healing

Shamballa 10 salutation

Shamballa 808 spring

Shamballa 707 summer

Shamballa 606 fall

Shamballa 202101 winter

Shamballa 94994 celestial, astrological, planetary and zodiac cleansing of negative influences

Shamballa 76767676 harmonization of opposites, good and bad, yin and yang, positive and negative

Shamballa 63 healing of the female energy and female aspect

Shamballa 73 healing of the male energy and male aspect

Shamballa 884 healing of the inner child

Shamballa 1111111111 child healing

Shamballa 222 animal healing

Shamballa 771 plant healing

Shamballa 8801 rejuvenation

Shamballa 7703 beauty

Shamballa 994 abundance

Shamballa 9910 financial independence and maturity

Shamballa 9912 financial empowerment and new openings

Shamballa 7771 etheric vitality, bioenergy, prana, chi, life-force energy healing

Shamballa 77 78 guardian angel

Shamballa 99 00 higher self

Shamballa 546474 loving kindness

Shamballa 1010 1111 1212 protection on all levels

Shamballa 8 protection SOS

Shamballa 07 21 healing SOS

Shamballa 10 protection

Shamballa 21 goal, aim

Shamballa 0011 heal the past

Shamballa 9900 heal the future

Shamballa 11 12 11 holographic and quantum healing and clearing

Shamballa 11 11 44 44 relaxation

Shamballa 8989 dreams

Shamballa 000 peaceful sleep

Shamballa 0000 dreams within the light

Shamballa 00000 sleep of the master

Shamballa 11117 spiritual, energetic, mental awakening

Shamballa 4567 emotional upliftment, recovery from sadness, negativity, grief, attachment

Shamballa 9900 success, if God wills it

Shamballa 0099 God is creating my life

Shamballa 80 I love God, I love the light, I love humanity, and I love to love.

Shamballa 7878 meditation

Shamballa 1 88 98 nutritional healing

Shamballa 0101 inner divine value, dignity, humility, return to innocence

Shamballa 99899 spiritual truth, overcoming illusions regardless of the cost

Shamballa 9898 rescue (rescue remedy)

Shamballa 4411 energy empowerment of a specific organ

Shamballa 4400 energy empowerment for all body systems

Shamballa 4477 empowerment for self-healing pro-cesses, instant healing, inner empowerment

Shamballa 447700 release, purification, regeneration (to overcome a disease)

Shamballa 4488 multiple-level healing

Shamballa 4949 increased energy flow

Shamballa 48888 9999 7777 healing involving materialization, dematerialization, transmutation, dense matter

Shamballa 7 801 angels of the highest first creative light

Shamballa 7 809 angels of meditation, connection, guidance, spiritual work, and healing

Shamballa 7 808 angels of love, peace, and joy

Shamballa 7 8000 angels of wholeness, good fortune, protection, and happiness

Shamballa 5555 optimal communication

Shamballa 5555 333 communication, peace, serenity, joy, clarity, patience

Shamballa 448844 independence, rights, strength

Shamballa 449 endurance

Shamballa 774 hope

Shamballa 776655331 forgiveness, release

Shamballa 008800 Shamballa initiation

Shamballa 110011 powerful energies of the source, the logos, and the spirit of the creative divine trinity

Shamballa 6600 work, purpose of life, divine intervention

Shamballa 6611 work, creativity, wholeness

Shamballa 6677 work, healing, energizing

Shamballa 6644 work, success, abundance, victory

Shamballa 6688 work, peace, harmony and balance

Shamballa 6699 work, completion, new beginning, guidance, delegation

Shamballa 3383 empowerment of friendship

Shamballa 3322 empowerment of creativity, strength, talents, self-confidence, and self-worth

Shamballa 3377 energetic empowerment, upliftment, rejuvenation

Shamballa 3366 empowerment of cleansing, spiritual mysteries, knowledge

Shamballa 3344 empowerment of manifestation, success, abundance

Shamballa 33 88 99 empowerment of love, attraction, passion, personal relationships, companionship

Shamballa 3310 empowerment of body

Shamballa 3312 empowerment of enlightenment and spirit

Shamballa 3313 empowerment of good fortune, synchronicity, flow

Shamballa 3388 empowerment of harmony, serenity, peace, freedom

Shamballa 3393 empowerment of joy and bliss

Shamballa 44 44 4 cellular body regeneration

Shamballa 983 forgiveness of the self and liberating consciousness from all kinds of negativity

Shamballa 6655 983 detachment from dependency and ill habits; purification of everyday life, substances, chemicals, and so on

Shamballa 6655 10 11 12 13 energetic protection from radiation, waves, smoke, pollution, radioactivity, chemicals, viruses, parasites, illnesses, electromagnetic-negative fields and factors of all kinds and of all intensities; purification of accumulated negativity and toxicity

Shamballa 787 Archangel Michael

Shamballa 789 Archangel Gabriel

Shamballa 780 Archangel Uriel

Shamballa 787 77 Archangel Raphael

Shamballa 789 99 Archangel Metatron

Shamballa 787 66 Melchizedek

Shamballa 787 88 Mahatma

Shamballa 787 88 99 Higher Self

Shamballa 11 787 88 99 00 I Am Presence, Infinite Source, God

Shamballa 6699 966 answers, messages, channeling

Shamballa 88 0 88 opening for healing

Shamballa 88 10 88 closing for healing, completion

Shamballa 66 77 88 healing of fear and phobias

Shamballa 779900 invocation to the spiritual laws and the divine rights

Shamballa 77 77 77 00 11 triple purifying, healing, and empowering shower of life-force energy, light, and love

Shamballa 66 99 balance of the energy centers (chakras)

Shamballa 66 99 11 22 33 44 55 66 77 balance of the energy bodies and of their elements

Shamballa 00 10 balanced and complete integration of the Shamballa Golden Codes within the body, the energy system, the mind, and the spirit

Shamballa 00 11 deeper grounding of the Shamballa Golden Codes

Shamballa 00 12 greater manifestation of the Shamballa Golden Codes on every level and for every occasion

Shamballa 00 11 11 22 immediate manifestation of the Shamballa Golden Codes and of their beneficial effects

Shamballa 00 11 22 33 44 55 66 77 harmonization and alignment of the person with the Shamballa Golden Codes on all levels

Shamballa 000000 purification, regeneration, and harmonization of all of the Shamballa Golden Codes

Shamballa 10 10 10 10 May the highest plan, the highest good, and the Divine Will prevail, Amen. Thank you!

Also by Georgios Mylonas (Geom!*)

Angelic Invocations

Angelic Symbols

Angelic Mysticism